The Official

Encyclopædia of the Cornish Pasty

Les Merton

Illustrated by Nicola Clark

To Mutti
Best Wishes
Les Merton

Palores Publications
Redruth - Kernow

THE OFFICIAL
ENCYCLOPÆDIA OF THE CORNISH PASTY

Text ©Les Merton 2003
Illustrations ©Nicola Clark 2003

ISBN 0 9539594 8 1

Published by

Palores Publications
1 Station Hill
Redruth
Cornwall (Kernow) TR15 2PP

Printed by

St. Ives Printing & Publishing Company
High Street
St. Ives
Cornwall (Kernow) TR26 1RS

Contents

Author's Notes

In *The Official Encyclopædia of The Cornish Pasty* I have included some Cornish dialect (written in italics). It is scattered throughout the book and, just like pepper in a pasty, it enhances the flavour.

Once again, I have tried to capture the sound of the dialect I love and remember by writing it phonetically. I believe this makes it easier for the reader. If read aloud the words sound and feel authentic.

Naw wat I mane do ee?

Ef yew doant, yew caan stull buy tha book cos et maakes a ansum pressant.

Please feel free to send any comments to me via:–

Palores Publications

Enjoy the book and more important, enjoy the pasties!

Les Merton

Warning: *This book is not recommended for bedtime reading. Some of our researchers have tried reading this book in bed and ended up in the kitchen making a pasty.*

Acknowledgements
This book would not have been possible without
the taste of Cornish Pasties.

Dedication
This book is for all seekers of the truth and pasty lovers
around the world.

History of the Pasty

The Garden of Eden

The Cornish Pasty has been with us since the beginning of time. Well almost! Contrary to popular belief, Eve wasn't tempted by an apple, but by a pasty. Apparently it was a very big pasty. Naturally Eve wanted to save a corner for *dreckly*. However Adam found the corner and ate it. I'm sure you know the rest . . .

8000 - 2700 BC

It is very evident that the pasty was in Cornwall 8000 - 2700 BC. Man depended on successful hunting to survive. Cave paintings have been found in Polfibber Caves with man chasing a stag, the stag would provide food, hides and bone. What is also very clear from these ancient drawings is that the woman made pasties from whatever meat her mate managed to kill. Polfibber Caves in west Cornwall have the only cave drawings to survive, that show a cave dwelling couple enjoying a pasty.

Author's note: Polfibber Caves were sealed in 1956 to preserve this piece of Cornish history for future generations. I am sworn to secrecy over their exact location.

5

Ancient Egyptian

Pasties have been the favourite food of all the greats of history. The pasty is well known as the food of the Pharaohs (3200 BC – AD 300). One of the main reasons that there was such dedication to the arts of building and sculpture, is the pasty. This rich wholesome meal, made with purpose bred sheep, cattle and antelope and with vegetables from the Nile valley, created such inspiration.

It is widely believed that the Pharaohs wrapped their pasties in papyrus to protect them from the scarab beetle.

At pasty banquets the guests of honour would be seated on high back chairs while others sat on simply made stools. Men and women were often separated at these functions. Most ate their pasties with their hands. Often bowls of perfumed water would be on the tables for the diners to rinse their fingers.

Ancient Greece

In ancient Greece pasty suppers were of a cultural nature. On these special social occasions the guests would enjoy music,

dancing and poetry. Often, great debates, such as 'Should the pasty be made with or without parsley?' would continue into the small hours.

Between 800 - 30 BC in Greece pasty banquets were usually all male affairs. It wasn't considered fitting for women to attend. However there was an exception to this rule and this was made for the *hetaerae* (educated courtesans who offered intellectual and artistic stimulus and, of course, the very thing to round off a pasty banquet.)

Ancient Rome

Between 753 BC - AD 476 Rome was noted for its food. The pasties were fit for the gods. Unfortunately many of the recipes were lost at Pompeii and Herculaneum. From coloured mosaics that survive we do know that dormice pasties were popular. The dormice were fattened in darkened jars on chestnuts and acorns.

Peacocks may also have filled a pasty or two in ancient Rome. The loss of the flying horse Pegasus has been attributed to the gluttonous nature of a drunken centurion who wanted a different filling for the pasties he had made for his men.

Dark Ages

During the dark ages, despite many declines, pasties were still eaten. It is believed they were consumed mainly at night.

Middle Ages

In mediaeval books there are lots of references to courtesy and there are many that are just for pasty eating. Often large pasties were shared by two people, who started at opposite ends and ate towards the middle. It was considered very bad manners to scratch your head or other parts when sharing a pasty.

Salt was the in thing; never take a pinch of salt with your fingers to flavour the pasty. Always dip your knife into the salt and sprinkle it from the knife.

Discoveries from the New Worlds

Potatoes were in. Many places in Great Britain enjoyed the delight of the Potato from the second half of the sixteenth century. In Cornwall, *tatties* as we called them, had been around hundreds of years. Our boys used to row across and bring back boat loads from the New World just to keep the pasty business booming. We just let others believe they discovered it all first, *lik yew do.*

17th Century

Forks came in and were very fashionable up country. We didn't go a lot on them (*stull doan't*). We carried on eating pasties with *bleeding* hands.

Tudor Banquets

Great days for a nosh up. Pasties were often served inside the mouth of a wild boar. During the feasts that happened on a regular basis, entertainment accompanied the pasty. It was provided by professional comedians and jesters, many of whom relied on a supply of pasty jokes to come top of the bill.

18th Century

Cornwall told the rest of the world about eating pasties with a cup of *suggery* tea. Tea became a best seller. By the middle of the 18th Century tea was the principal drink of all classes.

19th Century

Around 1823 the game of Rugby originated. This came about when Cornish students started throwing pasties to one another in a game of catch. Rival boys tried to snatch the pasties. Rugby was the game that developed. The ball was introduced within days of the first game as it seemed to be such a waste of a good pasty.

Victorian and Edwardian Years

The cult of the pasty spread. Mrs Beeton suggested pasty with everything and she recommended the pasty as the perfect picnic food. (Once again the Cornish said nothing about *croust or crib*). Mrs Beeton achieved her fame and said she enjoyed a pasty with champagne.

20th Century

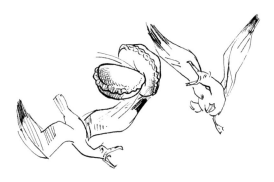

Prohibition! Pasties illegal in America! The gangster years start with bootleg pasties made in illicit Cornish ranges *(slabs)* up in the hills.

Man walks on the moon. It was a giant step for a man, who was *daggin* to get home for his pasty.

Remember the 11th minute of the 11th hour of the 11th day of the 11th month! Two pasties thrown in the air, for the seagulls, at St Ives eclipsed one another and the lights went out. This caused wide spread panic among the seagulls who thought it was a new method of culling.

21st Century

The first ever official Encyclopædia of the Cornish Pasty goes on sale.

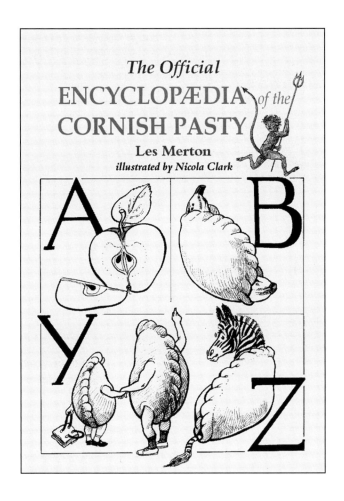

Author's Note: Valuation experts unanimously agree that this title *wull bay wurth a fort-chune en years ta cum.*

Making a real Cornish Pasty

Before you try this recipe, remember to get the best results, always use local organic vegetables and don't forget to buy from a local butcher selling Cornish beef. Ask for skirt, chuck or pasty meat.

The Pasty Recipe

Ingredients

for the pastry	*for the filling*
1 lb/450g plain flour	1 lb/450g meat of
5 oz/125g of lard	your choice
pinch of salt	1 lb/450g potatoes
drop of water to mix	1 lb/450g swede
	1 small onion
	1 oz/25g of butter
	bit of fresh parsley

How to do a proper job. Get the heat up round 400° F. Make the pastry the way Missus Laity would. Cut into two pieces. Roll it out, put a decent 10 inch dinner plate on each one and cut round it.

Cut up the potatoes and swede into small shaped pieces, chop up the onion as well. Now do the beef, cut it into small cubes about quarter inch, make sure you get rid of any fat in the beef.

Next one of Missus Laity's tricks of the trade. Put the rolling pin under one half of the pastry rounds. Layer your vegetables. Some say put the swede down first because its slower to cook, then potato, then onion.

Make your own mind up regarding the order you lay the veg down. Give it a pinch of salt and pepper. Add the meat with knobs of butter and the parsley, a bit more pepper *wull do-en gud.*

Now, comes the folding the pastry into the pasty shape. Takes years of practice to get it as good as Missus Laity.

Dampen the edges of the pastry, bring it up with floury hands. Pinch the edges together, then crimp the best you can. When you've done both pasties *put-en* in a floured tray and bake for about three quarters of an hour. And the best part comes next . . .

Now that you have read how to make a proper Cornish pasty, it is time to explore 'The Official Encyclopædia of the Cornish Pasty'.

Please note this book is unique. I would like to take this opportunity to thank Missus Laity (our supreme commander) and her team of grannies, mothers, wives and young maids who tried out all the recipes.

The author also benefited from our superb team of piskey researchers who burrowed deep into the underground vaults of Kresenn Kernow (The Cornwall Centre) to obtain much of the material for this book from secret archives.

In fact, everyone concerned with this project worked far beyond the call of duty.

Warning! None of the above, especially Missus Laity, will be held responsible for anything that happens to anyone who tries to profit from knowledge gained from reading this book.

Author's Note: When you read of the many variations of pasty, you will realise why the devil never dared cross the Tamar.

Boiled Pasty in Vegetable Broth

Boiled pasties are for real. They are still being made today and Penryn is noted for them. I am indebted to a Penryn resident (who wishes to remain anonymous) for this recipe –

Ingredients

Vegetables	Meat	Pastry
½lb carrots	1lb/450g brisket	2 oz/50g lard
half a swede	8oz/200g skirt beef	4 oz/100g plain
two onions		flour.
one leek		Mix into
two potatoes		a stiff dough
one cauliflower		Leave for 20
or cabbage		minutes.

To Make The Pasty

Roll out the pastry into a round disc shape. Put the beef, fine cut into strips, in the middle. Fold over and curl the ends together. Put into the fridge until the soup is ready.

To Make The Soup

Put brisket into a large sauce pan, add salt and pepper to taste. Slice carrots, swede, onion, leek and potatoes into small pieces. Again add salt and pepper to taste. Add water so the pan is half full. Bring everything to the boil, then simmer. Add cauliflower, cut in two halves, to the soup. Once this is done, put the pasty in resting it on the two halves of cauliflower. Keep cooking everything for another hour until cooked. <u>Do not stir.</u>

A to Z of PASTIES

Apple Pasty ~ Peel and thinly slice the apples, lay on the pastry, lightly sprinkle with brown sugar. In the blackberry season you can mix blackberries with the apple.

Apple 'n' Hinge Pasty ~ The lungs and heart of an animal make this pasty special.

Apple 'n' Spice Pasty ~ Prepare a pound of apples, as above, and lay them on the pastry. Add a couple of ounces of sugar, half a pound of currants, one teaspoon of ground mixed spice and a bit of fine chopped lemon peel. Seal the pasty and bake at a moderate temperature.

Apple 'n' Sultana Pasty ~ Roll out the pastry into tea-plate size rounds. Place sliced apple with a few sultanas, add sugar to taste, a touch of spice and a small knob of butter. Dampen edge, fold over, seal and crimp. It takes about 15 to 20 minutes to bake in a hot oven.

Arsenic Pasty ~ On Friday 26th August 1853 the 'Royal Cornwall Gazette' reported a wilful murder. The child of a miner named Pellow, from Harrowbarrow, Calstock, which had been buried for a fortnight was exhumed.

Upon examination the contents of the child's stomach contained sufficient arsenic to poison three people.

A verdict of wilful murder was returned against the child's mother and her lover, a man called Tregay. Mrs Pellow eloped with Tregay after the child's death. Mrs Pellow also tried to kill her husband shortly before this by putting arsenic in his pasty for croust down the mine.

   After eating some of the pasty Pellow became sick. He drank warm salt water and vomited the pasty up. A dog that had eaten the remainder died almost instantly. After a warrant had been issued, Mrs Pellow and Tregay were apprehended in bed together in St Austell.

B**acon 'n' Egg Pasty** ~ Use about three slices of streaky bacon that has had the rind removed, and one hard boiled egg with the shell removed. Dice the bacon, chop the egg, add parsley, salt 'n' pepper. Enjoy the aroma as it bakes.

Bacon 'n' Turnip Pasty ~ A very appetising combination.

Banana Pasty ~ *Stans ta reasun et must be gud fer ee, cos yew nevur see any weak gorillas.*

Beef Pasty ~ This is usually a tea plate size pasty. Cut the beef fairly fine. Cover one half of the prepared round of pastry. Salt and pepper to taste. Add a layer of sliced onion with a bit of parsley and a small knob of butter. Damp one edge, fold over and crimp. Egg wash and bake in a hot oven until brown. Turn oven off and leave for another ten minutes for best results.

Beef and Stilton Pasty ~ The Stilton gives the pasty its own unique flavour.

Bits Pasty ~ Bits★ is a herb that is believed to be found only in North Cornwall. Bits grows in hedges and on the cliffs. It has also been used for medicinal purposes.

★ *The identity of bits is still being researched.*

Measure out an equal amount of bits, parsley and early shallots, wash well. Add half this quantity with spinach, cut some slices of bacon into small pieces, add well beaten egg. Cut the bits, parsley and spinach up into small portions. Pour boiling water over them. Leave for half an hour then squeeze all the moisture out. Put this onto the pastry. Fine cut the shallots, add the bacon. Seal as normal, leave a small space to add the beaten egg. Finish crimping and bake.

Boiled Pasty ~ *Tez fer real!* See anonymous recipe page 16.

Broccoli Pasty ~ Boil the broccoli until it is nearly cooked, but still firm, strain it and put in to the pasty. Add a pinch of salt.

Broccoli and Sweetcorn Pasty ~ Broccoli and sweet corn in a cheese sauce make a tasty pasty filling. If vegetarian cheese is used it is ideal for those who don't want to eat any animal products.

C**arrot Pasty** ~ Never been invented.

Cheese and Bacon Pasty ~ This is another variation of cheese and onion. It has diced ham added to enhance the flavour.

Cheese and Mushroom Pasty ~ By using cheese not made with animal rennet this gives the vegetarian another satisfying meal.

Chicken Pasty ~ Cut up the chicken in small pieces, add like meat.

Cock-taal Pastay ~ *Missus Laity es a chapel gwain woman an sha ray-fuses to descuss tha engredeants ov cock-taal pasties.*

Cornbeef Pasty ~ Fresh cornbeef crumbled on top of potatoes, turnip, onions; and sealed inside a traditional pasty.

Corner of Pasty ~ The end of a pasty usually with an identifying letter of the owner on it, saved especially to eat *dreckly*. Often noted to be more tasty when its cold.

Curlew Pasty ~ *Maake sure yew pluck oall tha fevvurs ovv en. Clain un owt, stick a bit ov onion up that parson's nose. Bake un weth sum ov tha usual veg. Et ell go down a trate.*

Date Pasty ~ Use dates, that have been stoned for you. Fill up a medium size pasty with them. Egg or milk wash the pastry, bake in a hot oven for about 10 - 15 minutes until light brown. Date pasties are delicious with cream.

Didjan ~ Miners left a *didjan* (a small piece of pasty or morsel of food) for the knockers or the little people, to help ensure safety underground.

Dodo Pasty ~ These used to be very popular but I haven't seen one for years. I will do a bit of research on the Dodo pasty situation and write it up in time for the next edition of this book.

Egg Pasty ~ Dampen the edge of a saucer size bit of pastry, sprinkle on some chopped parsley. Lightly beat an egg in a glass, add a bit of salt and pepper. Pour the egg over the pastry. Make sure you seal it up quickly, before it gets away.

Elephant Pasty ~ The elephant pasty is the largest pasty in the world. Another amazing fact about elephant pasties is that they never forget who's eaten them.

F*actory Pasties* ~ *Missus Laity blaames tha uniyuns or waas et tha onions? Dreckly ev-ray-boday wull relise tant propur. We oall knaw yew caan't mass produce a real Cornish pastay.*

Fairy Pasty ~ Use only the youngest, lightest fairies. Gently detach their wings, place on top of the usual layered vegetables, bake as normal. (Cautionary note. Don't put too much pepper in a fairy pasty, if the fairy sneezes it will blow the top crust clean off.)

Fairies are reputed to have been great favourites with Sir Arthur Conan Doyle, author of 'The White Company' and creator of Sherlock Holmes.

One can't help wondering did he . . .

Ferret Pastay ~ *Et stinks ta igh evun, but et goes down propur. Thus wan es not fer tha faaint eart'd.* Warnun: *Bout ower aftur yew et tha ferret pastay, yew've tha ten-da-see ta want ta jump down rabbet oles.*

Fig Pastay ~ *Figs es wat we caall'd raisins. So a fig pastay es wan maade weth raisins.*

Fish Pasty ~ Use herring or mackerel. Simmer the fish until it is soft enough to lift from the bones. Let it cool, remove skin and bones, put it on the pastry rolled out for the pasty, add parsley and season. Bake as usual.

Frog Pasty ~ It is understood this originates from France. Rumour has it that they were going to make a French version of Toad in the Hole. First a frog was mistaken for a toad. Then things went from bad to worse. Eventually it ended up as a Frog Pasty.

Recent research suggests that this is where the term, 'frog in the throat' comes from. Further food for thought: does this answer the age old question of what happened to the frogs when Wendron boys went frogging on the dark, wet nights with only a tilly lamp and a sack for company? Were the frogs they caught exported for pasties?

Government **Health Warning** ~ Not applicable to Cornish Pasties.

Grass Pasty ~ A normal pasty with herbs added.

Gravy Pasty ~ A Gravy Pasty or a pasty with gravy is a new fangled idea. Missus Laity said, *'We doan't want nothun ta do widdun.'*

Gud Meal Pastay ~ *Thus es a propur pastay. Yew knoaw wat I mane, wan thet angs ovur tha side ov tha pla-ate, jus lik Mawthur use ta maake. Thus es garr -un-teed ta be a moast fitty n tot-ta-lay fillun dennur or suppur.*

Ham, **Leek and Cheese Pasty** ~ Another combination where the ingredients complement one another.

Herby Pasty ~ Equal portions of washed parsley, shallots,

spinach. Place on the pastry, add some slices of bacon cut into small pieces. Whisk up an egg. Pinch up the edges of the pastry, leave a hole to pour in the egg. Finish pinching it up and bake in the oven.

Hoggan ~ I quote from A K Hamilton Jenkins, 'Cornish Homes and Customs', 'a hoggan or lump of unleavened dough, in which sometimes was embedded a morsel of green pork'

Possibly this was one of the forerunners of today's pasty.

Hogs Pudding Pasty ~ Use your favourite butcher's Hogs Pudding skinned and cut up. Put it in the pasty instead of normal pasty meat.

I ce pasty ~ Ideal for hippies. It's cool man.

Ink pasty ~ The only evidence of an ink pasty was found on a used paper bag in Decky Bray's garden shed.

Insecure pasty ~ A pasty crimped on both edges. Usually made by an *in-comer* who thinks her pasty will fall apart if it's only crimped on one side.

J am Pasty ~ This is a smaller pasty, sometimes made with a bit of left over pastry. Just add your favourite jam, seal the pasty and bake it as normal.

Jurrassic Pasty ~ Made with the meat so old, you'll need to borrow false teeth to chew it.

K angaroo Pasty ~ Ideal for *croust* in the outback. Lots of Cousin Jennys stuff the pouch with onion.

Kidney Pasty ~ Some people like to put kidney in a pasty with the meat.

Lamb Pasty
~ Pasties can be made with lamb or mutton, parsley enhances the flavour.

Especially for *in-comers* to Cornwall, Missus Laity notes that these pasties can't be made by *mutton dress'd as lamb*.

Lamb and Mint Pasty ~ Tender lamb marinated in a mint sauce and layered over potatoes, swede and onion. The vegetables can also have a mint seasoning.

Licky Pastay ~ Cut off the green leek ends. Wash and slice the rest of it. Put on the pastry, add butter, season with a bit of salt and pepper. Just to make it different, put a bit of bacon in this as well.

Liver and Onion Pasty ~ Roll out the pastry to the size of a small plate. Place half the onion on the pastry. Cover with trimmed and thinly sliced liver (ox liver is best but other liver can be used). Season with salt and pepper. Cover the remainder with onion and seal in the normal way. Egg wash can be used if available.

Love-apple Pasty ~ The tomato was originally known as the love-apple. This was because tomatoes were thought of as an aphrodisiac. Tomatoes were used in pasties at weddings for the bride and groom. This was guaranteed to inflame the passions of the newly weds.

Maake tha moost ov et Pastay
~ A real dialect pasty from the days when nothing went to waste. This is a very savoury pasty and one of the few that uses precooked fillings. Take the left overs, cold boiled potatoes and turnip. Mash them well together with a knob of butter. Add salt and pepper to season.

Put this filling into saucer size rounds of pastry. Add another knob of butter and some parsley if desired. Moisten edge of pastry, fold over, crimp edge. Egg or milk wash. Bake in hot oven for about ten minutes. *See-un as yewr makun tha moost ov et, thus wan lik a lot ov pastays caan bay enjoy'd ot or cold.*

Mabyer Pastay ~ Cornish dialect for a chicken pasty.

Meat Pasty ~ This is a tea plate size pasty, made with just beef and a bit of parsley and onion added. One of my childhood memories of eating this pasty was to slice the top cover off which always had meat stuck to it, add a liberal amount of 'Bee-top' brown sauce to this and eat it before eating the base with another dollop to give it that saucy flavour. Mouth-watering.

Mawthur's Pastay ~ I've never met a Cornish person who knows anybody who can bake a *pastay* better than *es Mawthur.*

Microwave Pasty ~ *I knaw tha wurd microwave es swear-un. But I waas advis'd ta enclude et en tha book. See microwave es wan ov em new vag.*

Maake up wat evur pastay yew fancy or warm wan up thet's oall-ridy bak'd.

Now wat evur yew do maake sur yew ave sumthun ta ate. Micro-wave pastays are ridy en two shakes ov tha dicky duck's quack. But more en liklay yew well eeve et en tha bin, cos et cums owt sum-thun awful.

Onlay theng es ef yew git oald, an ta tha stage wen yew've got naw teeth, et mite do tha job.

Minced Meat Pasty ~ It's a shame, nowadays because of the cost of things, minced meat is in. However the revolution is on its way.

Mincemeat Pasty ~ Another filling for the bit of left over pastry, *et'll maake ee thenk et's Chressmas any daay ov tha week.*

Mouse Pasty ~ If anyone wet the bed after picking dandelions, a mouse pasty was the remedy to stop the bed wetting.

Mouth-organ ~ Slang for a pasty.

Not Another Pasty ~ This is an expression up-country people seem to use a lot. Being Cornish I can't figure out why they keep saying it.

Onion Pasty ~ A tasty alternative to sausage rolls or cheese patties. This ideal taster for picnic or buffet is a small pasty with an onion filling. Use 3 inch or 8 cm pastry rounds and fill with seasoned onion.

Organic Pasty ~ Just like the good old days. Its catching on fast- only the best, for the best meal in the world!

Origami Pasty. ~ Keep folding it, so that it gets smaller and smaller, until it finally disappears.
NB: Best done in the mouth.

Parsnip Pastay ~ *Caan't emagine et caan ee. Theer's naw such theng, es theer?*

Pea Pasty ~ The first peas of a season were used as another pasty filling and were very popular.

Peacock Pasty ~ Very much a seasonal meal. Only the very tender slices of peacock breast are used. A peacock pasty is often cooked

at barbecues. The tail feathers of the peacock are ceremoniously used like a fan to cool the pasty down before it is eaten.

Penguin Pasty ~ Best eaten when it's cold.

Phoenix Pasty ~ *Use ta be oall tha ra-age. Then fer sum unknaw'd reesun ev-ray time wan waas put en tha oven, tha pastay burn'd es-self owt. Theere waas nuthun left but ashes. Anywaay thay kept tha ashes en Trura Museum cos dreckly tha Phoenix wull rise agin an we'll be waiten fer un.*

Poldark Pasty ~ Just like the Poldark books by Winston Graham and the television series from the books – you can't wait for the next one.

Pork Pasty ~ Fresh pork, from a local butcher in a pasty, with potatoes and flavour added to it with onion, sage or thyme.

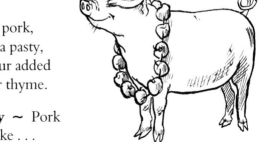

Pork and Apple Pasty ~ Pork and apple go together like . . .

Prune Pasty ~ *Thus wan wull kape ee regla.*

Quiet Pasty ~ A quiet pasty is one that shuts the mother-in-law, the *missus*, the kids, or the neighbours up for a bit while they're eating it. Ideal for that tranquil moment. Quiet pasties are often eaten before meditation by members of the *Gran Ordur ov Pastays*.

Rabbity Pastay~ Used to be very popular, especially in the days when many had to live off the land. Cut the fleshy part of the rabbit up small. Use instead of meat.

Rice Pasty ~ Cook rice in milk like you would for a pudding, sweeten and mix with an egg. Use a good short pastry. Fill with the cooked rice and bake until pastry is fairly well done.

Rook Pasty ~ This takes a bit of preparation. Skin the rook and cut up. Select the best of the breast and legs, soak overnight in slightly salted milk and water. Put into a prepared pasty with rashers of bacon on top of the rook.

Sausage Pasty ~ Use sausage meat or take the skin off your favourite banger and use the insides instead of meat. A palatable change.

Shallot Pasty ~ A great small pasty. Similar size to the onion pasty but with a tender young shallot filling.

Shirgar Pasty ~ Only one thing you can say about a Shirgar (the racehorse) Pasty. *Et's a winnur!*

Snakey Pastay ~ *Thus es ide-ale ef yew'r feelun a trif-full teasy.*

Sour Sauce Pasty ~ It's a very old recipe. Get a few sorrel leaves. Shrink by pouring boiling water on them. Spread a thin layer of leaves in a pasty.

Spicy Vegetable Pasty ~ A wide range of vegetables that include peppers, green beans, onion, swede, garlic, kidney beans and potatoes mixed in a spicy sauce of tomato, soy, ginger and chilli. It warms the cockles of your heart on a winter's day.

Squab Pasty ~ Squab means young pigeon. Some regard these as not being very tasty; its marvellous however, what the magic of a pasty with a good mix of traditional vegetables can do.

Star-Gazey Pastay ~ *Wan ov Mawthur's spechalls. Clain a herring. Put a bit of stuffun same as yew ave weth mabyers. Saw en up en tha middle weth a niddle an cotten. Put tha prepared herring en tha middle ov a bit ov roll'd owt daugh. Ave tha ead stick-un owt wan end an tha tail owt tha othur. Baken up propur. Eat tha lot obem, eyes un oall. Tis ansum!*

Steak and Ale Pasty ~ *Decky Bray sweers by et, special-lay wen ee's down tha pub.*

Steak Pasty ~ Eight ounces of steak in a pasty, done proper with the steak cut up, not minced.

Streaky Pork Pasty ~ Spread the pastry out thick and make a hollow for the number of servings. Fill the hollows with chopped streaky pork, salt well and bake. The juices settle in the bottom of the hollows and the top is brown and crispy. Sounds good. Tastes better.

Summur Pastay ~ *Nothur new wan. Got differunt culler peppurs en un. Tha idea cums fram cross tha waatur.*

Suggery Tay weth a Pastay ~ *Now yer talkun, weth wurds, naw gud avun a pastay weth owt a dish ov suggery tay ta washun down. Goes tagethur lik? Wull yew knaw cos yew ave tried un, avent ee.*

*T*attie Oggie ~ *Gud dialect wurd fer a pastay. Whech geeve us tha grate pat-re-otic, Oggie, Oggie, Oggie. Oi, Oi, Oi. Oggie . . .*

Thrashun Pasty ~ This is a giant of a pasty, an essential part of the farm worker's way of life. It was deliberately made extra large, served hot at midday and they had half later when it was cold. The perfect meal for harvest work in the field.

Tiddy Hoggan - Tiddy Hoggy ~ *Nothur naame fer a tatty pastay.*

Treacle Pasty ~ Inside the pastry it is as black as thunder. Treacle pasties are unique to Cornwall. A special heat resistant treacle that is only harvested in leap years from Bal Dryakel. Specially trained *denbals* go down deeper than Dolcoath to mine rich treacle.

The veins through which the treacle runs are mined by first of all twisting a treacle fork anti-clockwise into the vein carrying the thick liquid. Once the liquid is flowing it is collected in silver treacle buckets, so the quality won't be impaired. The treacle buckets are taken to the surface in three legged wheelbarrows. This black gold is stored in large vats, under armed guard, for five years until it matures enough to make Treacle Pasties. Highly recommended.

T-T Pasty ~ Initials are often put on pasties by making letters out of pastry. This identified who the pasty was made for and in some cases the owner, when a corner pasty was left for *dreckly*. Letters were also put on pasties to identify the contents for the varying tastes within a family. One lady always used to put the letters T – T on every pasty. When asked why she said: 'This T – T stands for *Tis Turnip* and that T – T stands for *Tiddun Turnip*'. Makes sense to me.

Turnip Pasty ~ Turnip can be used on its own for a pasty filling. Dice the turnip fine. Add plenty of pepper and a good size lump of butter to it. Bake the mix in the pastry. Eat it while it is hot.

In 'Portrait of Cornwall' – Claude Berry suggests splitting a hot turnip pasty while it's hot and spreading the contents with cream.

Twickenham Pasty ~ *Jus tha job ta hang un tha crossbar so our boays naw we're behind um oall tha waay. Oggie, Oggie, Oggie! Brings a lump ta yewr throat n tears to yewr eyes yo.*

Unique Pasty ~ A proper Cornish pasty is unique and it can only be made in Cornwall by a good Cornish woman.

Up-Country Pasty ~ Sorry! – Politely based on Missus Laity's comments: – Our readership includes a large number of Methodists. Therefore it would be very unfitting to comment on pasties made up-country.

Vegetable Pasty ~ Roll out the pastry as normal to the size required. Fill with layers of onion, turnip and potatoes. Make sure you add the seasoning as you go. Fold and seal the pastry. Cook as normal. For that touch of class, make a small hole in the middle of the top of the pastry just before serving and dribble in a small measure of thin cream.

Veggie Pasty ~ Just the job for vegetarians. One of the traditions that seem to have started with veggie pasties is to make them with wholemeal pastry. Obviously all animal by-products are out. Made properly a real veggie pasty with traditional organic vegetables is delicious.

It is worth noting that soya mince or crumbled vegetable burger can be added to the vegetables selected for another version of the veggie pasty.

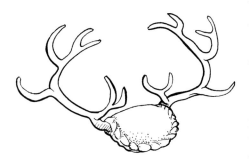

Venison Pasty ~ This was a classic 18th century meal. Venison was baked with neck of mutton and red wine. When it was tender it was covered in puff pastry and baked until the pasty was brown and well risen.

Veryan Pasty ~ These pasties are unique just like the famous round houses at either end of the village of Veryan. Some say, a local vicar built these round houses so the devil couldn't hide in the corners. Nothing quite so sinister with Veryan pasties; they are made round, purely so the succulent juices will not settle in one corner of the pasty.

Vice Pasty ~ the oldest food in the world, made by ladies from the oldest profession in the world.

Vindaloo Pasty ~ *Loo es about right,* (specially after you have eaten one.) It's hot going in, and definitely hotter coming out.

Vitamin Pasty ~ Vitamin pasties, these contain all the essential ingredients of a pasty and are available in tablet or capsule form. It is believed that both the Americans and the Russians gave their space explorers these pasty vitamin pills on recent expeditions. Currently these are only available on the black market, even if you pay over the odds, it may be worth it. A note of warning! Pasty vitamins are addictive.

Windy Pasty ~ It's not what immediately comes to mind. Windy pasty is that left over bit of pastry, rolled out, folded over and crimped. It's then baked in the oven. When it's done and while it's still hot, open it out flat with a knife. Fill each side with butter or jam. Windy pasties can be eaten hot or cold. *Ansum.*

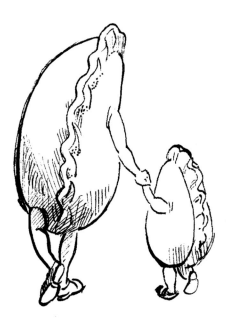

Xtacy Pasty ~ *Ver-ray poplar weth tha youngsters. Et es wick'd. Jus tha job fer a rave.*

Xzackly Rite ~ A pasty that's made *propur* just like the pasties *Mawthur* bakes every day. *Xzackly rite.*

Young Pasty ~ Cornish born and bred call a small pasty, under four inches, a young pasty.

***Z**am-zoodled Pastay* ~ A pasty that is half cooked or over cooked. *Corse wan cud gaar-un-tay who et wud bay maade by.*

Zebra Pasty ~ Make the same as normal. Please <u>make sure</u> the stripes run from left to right, <u>not</u> top to bottom. Zebra pasties with the meat stripe running from top to bottom are as tough as an old boot.

Zelah Pasty ~ The original Zelah Pasties recipe is copyright to Missus Polwiddle and she wants royalties to print it. *Tha maan-age-ment* believes this book would have a limited sale at £100 per copy, so we decline Mrs Polwiddle's offer.

Zulu Pasty ~ I was going to provide a Zulu Pasty recipe. However, after seeing the film 'Zulu'. I thought, *'Thay doan't dayserve a pastay aftur tha waay thay trat'd ur boays.'*

***ZZZ**at's et* ~ *Pastay time.*

In Cornwall pasties are everywhere: in children's games, girls bake and feed pasties to dolls, boys draw pasty shaped towns with chalk or with their boots heels to play games of marbles.

MARBLES

Around this *'pasty shape town'*

begs furst or *begs last*
is settled before tactics and rules like,

deads, kills, changers or even worse
no deads, no kills, no changers are laid down.

Before, *toeing the line,* there's the choice,
a *no going back on* choice; *keeps* or *poors.*

Pinkeying up requires a knack, get as close
as possible to *town,* without becoming *dead.*

With your best *alley* (at least a *twelver)*
between finger and thumb, kneel,

beg a move if you have to, take aim,
fire but don't *funkey...*

Funkeying can lead to, *cheat, cheat never beat.*
It could mean your *clayers* are bombed,

by giant *steelies,* (out of whopping machines
that Johnny Pascoe's dad has never heard of).

Naw Pastays Tadaay

Decky Bray, tha odd job mahn, ate es croust earlay. Cum denner time, ee waas starvun, ee felt ee cud ate a oss an cart an chase tha drivur.

See-un ee waas workun up tha rawd fram Missus Laity's Tay Room, Decky set ov down tha rawd lik a long dog. Ee got theer en naw time. Ee wen enta tha Tay Room an strate up ta tha countur an sid, "I'll ave a pasty ef yew plaise Missus Laity."

"Theer's naw pastays tadaay." Missus Laity rayplied.

"Gis on, yew ave pastays evur-ray daay." Decky sid.

Missus Laity fold'd er arms an sid, "I'm tellun yew theer's naw pastays tadaay Decky!"

"But, yew ave pastays ever-ray daay." Decky ensist'd.

Missus Laity waas gitten a bit teasy weth Decky by thus time, "Watch me lips!" sha shout'd. "Theer's naw P-A-S-T-F-I-E-S tadaay."

Decky shout'd bahck. "Few yew'r en-form-a-shun theer's naw 'F' en pastays."

"Zackly wat I sid!" exclaim'd Missus Laity.

37

Cornish Pasties – Amazing Facts!

Tyrannosaurus Rex was the largest carnivorous reptile of the dinosaur period. A single bite of food, possibly taken out of another dinosaur, would give a human family of four enough meat to make pasties for a month.

If the eucalyptus tree was to become extinct, the koala would become extinct too. If the pasty was to disappear overnight, the Cornish would . . . (Sorry, I can't continue this line of reasoning. It is upsetting Missus Laity.)

Most Cornish people, like everyone else by the age of sixty, have lost 40 percent of their ability to smell and 50 percent of their taste buds. Yet they can still enjoy the traditional pasty.

Writing under the pseudonym Lewis Carroll, English mathematician, Charles L Dodgson coined dozens of new nonsensical words in Alice in Wonderland, Through the Looking Glass and his nonsensical poems. Many of these became part of the English language. Missus Laity came up with, 'crousty'. (*Author's note:* Watch this space.)

The word 'million' didn't come into being until around 1300. Until then, the largest number word was 'myriad', which was Greek for 10,000. Archimedes in calculating the number of poppy seeds in the entire universe as he knew it, used expressions meaning 'myriads of myriads of myriads . . .' Missus Laity when thinking about the number of pasties consumed since the beginning of time came up with, 'Pastions of pastions of pastions . . .'

In his early days, Picasso kept warm by burning some of his drawings. Missus Laity wants it to be known she has never burnt a drawing or a pasty in her life.

Paper bags were first made by hand in 1850. Bessie Jenkin (Bessie Trenear that was) became the first person to put a pasty in a paper bag in 1851. Bessie won three empty paper bags in a competition organised by the Inventors Union to find a use for new inventions. The first bag she tried to carry some hot coals in

proved unsuccessful. The second bag she took down to the village pump to fetch some water home, it leaked like a basket. The third bag she popped a pasty in to hide it from her husband, who smelt the pasty in its hiding place within seconds and proceeded to eat the pasty from the bag. Pasties in paper bags became a way of life. The first automatic bag-making machine was invented in 1876. A point of interest – pasties are still made by hand.

Betty Grable was Hollywood's highest paid star for a while and was known to have the most highly insured legs. Missus Laity, due to star in the forthcoming film 'The Official Encylopædia of the Cornish Pasty', has had her crimping fingers insured for £5,000,000.

The biggest selling book in America is Noah Webster's Blue-Backed Speller published in 1783. In revised editions it is still in print and has sold well over 100 million copies. Very quickly catching this up in America is, 'Instructions For Eating A Cornish Pasty' by Decky Bray.

I like to include the following poem in my act, when I do performance poetry or a Cornish evening. I always ask the audience to join in with the refrain. Everyone has great fun joining in. Why not try it at home with family and friends.

A Cornish Custom

Et doant mathur
wethur yew eat
et mid-daay or noon,
wethur yew saay
croust or crib.

Wan theng fur sure pastay fer denner
es rite an prophur, cos tez a Cornish custum.

Et doant mathur
wethur yew eattun
weth a knife n fork
or owt ov a bag,
wethur tha mate
es skirt or chuck.

Wan theng fur sure pastay fer denner
es rite an prophur, cos tez a Cornish custum.

Et doant mathur
wethur yew layer
or mix tha veg,
wethur tha tatty
es sliced or cubed.

Wan theng fur sure pastay fer denner
es rite an prophur, cos tez a Cornish custum.

Et doant mathur
wethur tez turnip or swede,
weth or wethowt parslay,
wethur tez crimp'd
un tha top or tha side.

Wan theng fur sure pastay fer denner
es rite an prophur, cos tez a Cornish custum.

Et doant mathur
wethur et's ome maade
or owt ov a shop,
wethur tez ole fashun
weth wan end savoray
an tha othur end sweet.

Wan theng fur sure pastay fer denner
es rite an prophur, cos tez a Cornish custum.

Et doant mathur
wether yew ate
yewr pastay hot or cold,
wethur yew knaw zackly
wat I'm gwain ta saay nixt.

Wan theng fur sure pastay fer denner
es rite an prophur, cos tez a Cornish custum.

The Cornish Highwayman

Deck Turnip was a Cornish highwayman. He used to hold up stagecoaches with a shout of, '*Staand n day-liv-ur!*' Deck would rob the stagecoach passengers of all their gold, silver and valuables. The only reason the feats of Deck Turnip, Cornish Highwayman extraordinaire are not in the history books; no-one ever complained about him.

Before he rode off with the loot, Deck Turnip used to give everyone he robbed one of his mother's pasties. It was great value for money.

Corners of Pasties

Greeting

A Cornish greeting, when you saw someone eating a pasty in their hand was, *'Who's cut yer hand?'* or *'Yewr hand es bleedun!'*

Miners and Their Pasties

The pasty is the traditional meal for a Cornish miner working underground. Miners took a pasty down the mine for their *croust,* in a clean linen bag. Some of these bags had drawstring tops. If a miner had his pasty in a paper bag, he would feel his wife was letting him down.

It has been said that miners held their pasties by the thick crimped edge like a handle to eat. Perhaps this handle, dirtied by working hands, was the *didjen* left to appease the *knockers.*

Fishermen and Their Pasties

Cornish fisherman, like all Cornish, love pasties; however it was considered bad luck to take a pasty to sea with them.

The Fastest Pasty in the West

The record for the world's fastest pasty is held by Jan Polwiddle. On the April 1st 1908, he had a pasty that travelled over one hundred miles an hour. What happened was, Jan dropped his pasty down Geevor shaft.

Missus Laity Sid

'Ef thay evur ded find Jan's pastay, dawhn tha bottum ov Geevar, they'll naw, Missus Polwiddle bak'd et cos et woan't be scat up.'

What Came First?

Question: What came first, the paper bag or the knife and fork to help the gentry eat their pasties?
  Answer: *Matthur do et.*

Go To Hell

The Devil stood outside of the gates of hell. 'Welcome Sam,' he said, with a wicked grin, to the new arrival.

'It took me ages to get here,' Sam said. 'I'm starved; my stomach feels like my throat's been cut. Is there a baker's shop?'

The Devil scratched his head. 'Of course,' he replied.

'Do they sell pasties?' Sam asked.

The Devil gave a wicked laugh, 'Course not! You're in hell!'

The Tastiest Part

Questun: Wat es tha tas-tay-est part ov a pasty?
  Furst ans-sur: Ef yew'r ating et owt of a bag, tha tasty part es tha laast cornur wheere oall tha juices ave run to.

Sec-con ans-sur: Ef yew're ating obem weth a knife n fork, tha furst mouthful es tha tastay-est cos yew've ad ta wate while yew cutten up ta gitten inta yer mouth.

Thurd ans-sur: Matthur do et.

Marquis de Sade

The Marquis de Sade was known for his cruelty. When he was asked to serve pasties for lunch. He looked wicked and said, 'No!'

Train Journey

A young lady boarded a train at Trelie Station and sat down in a compartment where the only other occupant was Jan Polwiddle.

As soon as the young lady sat down Jan Polwiddle said, *'Scuse me my ansum . . .'*

'If you speak again or annoy me I'll pull the communication cord!' the young lady snapped.

Jan Polwidddle didn't give up, he made several attempts to speak to the girl. Every time Jan uttered a word the girl threatened to pull the communication cord.

Jan gave up, when the train pulled into his station stop. He said, *'Yew caan pull tha cord ef yew waant, but stand up ta do et, then I caan git my pastay whech yew've bin sat un since yew got en.'*

Artiste's Pasties

According to, 'The Book of Euphemism' by Judith S Neaman and Carole G Silver, Artiste's Pasties are small breast shields glued on to the nipples by striptease artistes or exotic dancers. Rumour has it, Decky Bray tried to eat them, when they were still attached to a young female entertainer, at the Polwiddle Men's Institute Annual Stag Show.

Know Your Own Pasty

It is a custom to put an initial or a mark for each member of the family on one end of the pasty. Not only does this identify the pasty but the filling can be made to order.

Tradition insists that you eat your pasty by holding it in your hand, and starting it from the opposite end to the initial or mark. That way, if a few leave a corner of the pasty for a bit later on, there will be no argument as to whose it is because the end that is left will have an initial or mark on.

Pasties by Donkey Cart

In those so-called good old days a lady used to collect pasties in bags with the owners' names on from the village of Troon and take these into Camborne for the Holman's workers' lunch.

Pasties by Bus

In the 1950s and '60s, a bus used to start in Penryn and, via Old Hill in Falmouth, make its way to Falmouth Docks. The bus conductor would pick up pasties from the housewives put them in a basket and deliver them to the husbands working at Falmouth Docks in time for their lunch.

Many housewives in this area were also asked to bake pasties for seamen from ships in the dock yard, who wanted to taste the savoury meal after smelling it.

Pasties by Train

Many expatriate organisations like the London Cornish have had pasties sent up by train from back home for their get togethers.

Plaise Bay-leeve me

Fer oall ov ee thet wans ta see tha werld, doan't evur, nevur evur, spect ta git a Cornish Pastay owtside ov Cornwall.

Ef yew caan't work thet wan owt, et mite pay ee ta stay down ere a bit longer.

Early Pasty

A K Hamilton Jenkins is a writer of great repute. In his book, 'Cornish Homes and Customs' I would like to refer to what is perhaps the earliest reference to pasties in the 18 century.

'The labourers in general bring up their families with only potatoes or turnips, or leeks or pepper grass, rolled up in a black barley crust, and baked under ashes.'

Famous Quotes

Good luck to all the Cornish booys
That niver yet was baiten
A pastay may they niver want
Nor stummicks for to ait'n.

A K Hamilton Jenkins, 'Cornwall and its People'

Faithur lik'd mate n tatte best
Mawthur lik'd turmutt n mate
Bouy Jack wantus oall mate
Boy Tom lik'd lickey best
Tha maids edden ticular toall.

Anon

Fruit and Nut Case

The case for fruit and nut pasties applies to oranges. Large oranges were split into segments and offered as an orange pasty. Brazil nuts are known as pasty nuts.

Crimping Advert

Seen recently in the Polwiddle Times newspaper: Spare set of false teeth for sale or hire. Ideal for crimping pasties. Apply, Decky Bray, The Shed, (opposite that phone box), Polwiddle, or ring the phone box.

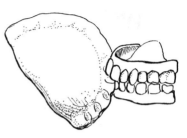

Devil of a Job

It has been said that the Devil never crossed the Tamar into Cornwall, because Cornish women are known for putting anything in a pasty.

They reckon the Devil isn't brave enough to risk coming into Kernow, he's afraid how he might end up.

When the Pasty Shops are Shut

On a day like today
when the pasty shops are shut

there will never be tomato sauce
given away in packets of cornflakes

or crisps pickled in goat's milk
and sold in jars with a flip top lid

Vincent van Gogh won't be taking
photographs with a Polaroid

and Jesus won't be driving around
with a fish logo on his transit van

I can't imagine Michael Jackson lasting
the whole day without looking in a mirror

neither can I see the invisible man
being given a good seeing to

now that the mobile phone
has replaced the comfort blanket

poetry can be spoken anywhere
to delight eavesdroppers anonymous

but on a day like today
when odd socks are colour co-ordinated

its not worth getting out of bed
or putting full stops after anything

Pasties

Pasties?

You said talk about something,
instead of having my head stuck behind the paper.

Why Pasties?

We've been married for thirty years,
every day we've had Pasties for lunch.

I know that but you can't talk
about Pasties as conversation can you?

Of course you can.

How?

Well you keep making different sizes.

Only because I like variety.

See, conversation!
Some people say – yesterday's Pasties –
meaning its over and done.

Oh, I see what you mean.

Before we was married
I once had flowers in my Pasty.
That was when I was a Hippy.

I never knew you was a Hippy.

Pasty Sports

Pastay n Fork Raace

Contestants spear a pasty with a fork and run to the finishing line. If a contestant drops their pasty they must go back to the starting line and start again. First one over the line wins and gets to eat all the pasties.

Pastay Pitchun

Contestants spear a pasty with a pitch fork and try to *eeve* it over a cross bar which increases in height with each round of the pitching. Contestants are eliminated when their pasty fails to clear the cross bar. The winner is the pasty pitcher who pitches the highest pasty.

Pastay Relay Raace

Each team has four runners who run 100 yards each. The runners pass a pasty to the next team member (in the same way a baton is passed in a country relay race). If the pasty is dropped or breaks, the team responsible must eat the pasty before continuing. This race has been discontinued in many parts of Cornwall because of the cost of supplying pasties. The last pasty relay race was never finished, and even then 40,031 pasties were consumed before bad light stopped play.

Pastay en the Sack Raace

Each Pasty is put into a separate hessian sack. These are left in the middle of a field. The pasty owners then wait to see which pasty is devoured first by trained, blindfolded pasty worms.

Pass tha Pastays

When the music stops take a bite of the pasty being passed around. (**Author's note**: Lots of cheating goes on with this noble sport.) When the music stops and there is no pasty to eat that person is declared the winner. But what has really been lost to gain this doubtful honour?

Land's End to John 0'Groats Cornish Pasty Eating Marathon

This is the only unsuccessful Land's End to John O'Groats event. It has never been completed. Whenever anybody has crossed over the Tamar eating a pasty, they have turned back to Cornwall, as soon as they have finished eating it.

John 0'Groats to Land's End Cornish Pasty Eating Marathon.

This event – is a non-starter.

Pasty Hurling

This ancient Cornish sport is staged on February 30th each year at Trewossnum. A pasty made by the oldest inhabitants of Trewossnum is thrown from the Mace Bearer's window into the hungry mob and there's *ell ta paay*.

Pasty Records

Pastays en a Mini

School children from Trelie Junior school put 304,987,789 pasties into a mini before the chassis gave way.

Pastay un top ov Mount Everest

The first Cornish Pasty reached the top of Mount Everest on the 14th February 1931. It was carried up there, after five previous attempts failed, by Cornish Mountaineer I B Damned.

Tha Fastust Ascent ov Mount Everest

Cornish Mountaineer, I B Damned, climbed Mount Everest in 3 minutes 31 seconds on 15th February 1931 to retrieve the pasty he had left there the day before.

Tha Longust Pastay en tha Werld

This is still being measured. So far 1000 miles of pasty have been measured stretching from Land's End to John O'Groats. The pasty shoots off the end of Scotland and disappears over the horizon. An expedition which set out to continue measuring it failed to return. It is believed, they ran out of supplies and are eating their way back.

Tha Hottest Pastay Evur

The hottest pasty ever was cooked in the volcano on top of Mount Etna on the 1st April 2000. A temperature of *'by gad thet's hot'* was recorded by Cornish scientist Howie Dohun.

Tha Oldest Pastay Evur

The oldest pasty ever was two minutes and ten seconds old. Decky Bray had a puncture in the front wheel of his bike and was two minutes and ten seconds late getting home for his dinner.

Tha Moast Poplur Pastay Name

Propur is the most popular pasty name ever, followed closely by *ansum*.

Tha Moast Poplur Pastay Tune

'Trelawny' is the most popular song to listen to when eating a pasty.

The Largest Number of Pastays Hidden

Caan't say – we're stull lookun fer um.

Record Number of Ponies Down a Mine

On Thursday 7th March 1831 it was estimated that there were over 4,000 ponies down in Bal Oss. All the pit ponies were taken down inside pasties.

The Most Beautiful Pasty in the World Ever

This work of art was modelled on the hourglass figure of Missus Laity in her corset.

The Ugliest Pasty in the World Ever

This travesty of a pasty was modelled on the figure of Missus Laity 'au naturel'.

Author's note: Without her corset.

Quotations

With a little more thought perhaps these worthy people could
have said:

Shakespeare
> 'My pasty, my pasty. My kingdom for a pasty.'

William Blake
> 'A fool sees not the same pasty that a wise man sees.'

Kipling
> 'You've eaten more pasties than I,
> Gunga Din.'

Winston Churchill
> 'Give us the pasties and we'll
> finish the job.'

Decky Bray
> *'Ate a pastay a daay ta kape tha flies et*
> *bay.'*

Henry Ford
> 'You can have any pasty you like,
> as long as it's a Cornish one.'

Shelley
> 'Hail to thee, blithe pasty.'

Jan Polwiddle
> *'Ate a pastay en a alf en a daay en a alf,*
> *en et wull be Satdaay en nixt ta naw time.'*

Longfellow
> 'Something attempted something done
> Has earned a night's pasty.'

Julius Caesar
'Beware of the eyes in pasties.'

Milton
'Pasty eaten, Paradise found.'

Virginia Woolf
'A pasty of one's own.'

Beau Brummell
'What's in your fat pasty.'

Homer
'Wait, a pasty has escaped the
barrier of thy teeth!'

Lord and Lady Hyphen-Dash-Hyphen
Lord: 'What's this one is having for lunch, my Lady?'
Lady: 'Its a Cornish Pasty, my Lord.'
Lord: 'Is this what the Cornish eat for lunch?'
Lady: 'It is, my Lord.'
Lord: 'Its far too good for them.'

Winston Churchill
'We shall eat pasties on the beaches,
We shall eat pasties on the landing grounds,
We shall eat pasties in the fields and in the streets,
We shall eat pasties in the hills,
We shall always eat pasties.'

Missus Laity
*'Theer's onlay wan ray-sun thet nawbody es call'd, Pastay en
Cornwall. Ef theer waas sumbody call'd, Pastay, everay time
yew shout'd to em, all tha rest wud thenk et waas croust time
an down tools, so naw work wud git dun.'*

Lenin
'Is it true that a pasty is so precious -
so precious that it must be rationed?'

Emily Bronte
> 'Riches I hold in light esteem
> And love I laugh to scorn;
> And lust of fame was but a dream,
> That vanished with the pasty.'

King Louis XV
> 'I shall award the pasty a blue ribbon.'

Baroness Orczy
> 'We seek them here, we seek them there,
> We seek them pasties everywhere.'

Walter Scott
> 'Come weal, come woe,
> We'll gather and go
> And live or die with a pasty.'

Thomas Grey
> 'What female heart can despise a pasty?
> What cat's averse to fish?'

Elizabeth Browning
> 'And kings crept out again to eat the pasty.'

Robert Burns
> 'O, what a picnic's in thy pasty.'

Tennyson
> 'A happy bridesmaid makes a happy pasty.'

Wordsworth
> 'She gave me eyes, she gave me ears;
> And humble cares, and delicate fears;
> A heart, the fountain of sweet tears
> And love, and thought, and a pasty.'

Keats
'Ever let the fancy roam,
Pasties are always in the home.'

Bill Clinton
'I did not eat that woman's pasty'.

Hilary Clinton
'And neither did I!'

Monica Lewinsky
'This feels like a pasty.
This looks like a pasty.
This doesn't taste like a pasty.'

Lord Nelson
'Give us a bite of your pasty,
Hardy.'

Shakespeare
'Friends, Romans, Cornishmen,
Lend me your pasties.'

King Alfred
'Gud job I burnt tha caakes n not tha pastays.'

Robert Louis Stevenson
'Fifteen men on the Dead Man's Chest
Yo-ho-ho and a Cornish Pasty
Eat and the Devil has done for the rest
Yo-ho-ho and a Cornish Pasty.'

Sherlock
'Elementary, my dear Watson.
My plate is empty . . .
You were the only person in the room.
It is obvious you ate the pasty.'

Elvis Presley
'The pasty of my best friend.'

George Washington
'Father, I cannot tell a lie
I did eat the pasty.'

Adolf Hitler
'The trains are running to time-
soon we'll have pasties.'

Malcolm X
'I had a pasty.'

Mae West
'Come up and have a pasty some time.'

The Fairy Godmother
'You will have a pasty, Cinderella.'

Franklin Roosevelt
'I pledge you – I pledge myself
to a pasty for the American people.'

Thoreau
'The man is the richest whose pleasures
are in the pasty.'

David Frost
'That was the pasty, that was.'

King Arthur
'Ded yew thraw thet pastay enta tha laake?'

Francis Drake
'The Spanish will have to wait. It's *croust* time an I must
finish my pasty before it gets cold.'

Lady Macbeth
'Is that a pasty I see before me?'

John Lennon and Yoko Ono

♩ All we are saying – give pasties a chance ♪

Glossary

alley	glass marble
bal	mine
clayers	clay marbles
clain	clean
crib	meal break
crimp	join the pastry ends of a pasty
crouse, croust	meal break
daggin	longing
daugh	dough
denbal	miner
denner	dinner
didjan	small piece of pasty or morsel of food
doan't	don't
dreckly	later
dryakel	treacle
fevvers	feathers
fi-er	fire
funkey	cheating move
funkeyin	moving your hand forward before firing
furst	first
giant steelies	large ball-bearings
gwain	going
gud	good
gis on	get on
kapes	keeps
knockers	little people who worked the tin mines (folk lore)

long dog	greyhound
mabyer	chicken
mahn	man
mane	mean
naw vag	new thing, new fashion
niddle	needle
pastay	pasty
pinkey-un-up	first throw
plaise	please
poast	post
rawd	road
scat-up	broken
slab	Cornish range/oven
steelies	ball bearings
teasy	bad tempered
theng	thing
thrashun	threshing (harvest)
trate	treat
uniyon	unions
zackly	exactly
zam-zoodled	half cooked or over cooked

Les Merton

Cornish personality, Les Merton, is a prolific writer. He is the author of: *Cornflakes and Toast* – poetry, *Missus Laity's Tay Room* – dialect, *The Spirit of a King* – the story of the Cornish Chough and *Light The Muse* – poetry also recorded on a CD.

Poetry and Cornish dialect are his passions. His poetry has been published in twelve different countries and he has won numerous awards for writing.

Photograph: John Berryman

Photograph: John Berryman

Nicola Clark

Multi-talented Nicola is a portrait artist, illustrator, singer songwriter, musician and a founder member of Kulture Brake, the St Ives Review group.

Her first CD, *Things to Sing About,* which includes an illustrated book of lyrics, is currently on sale. She is working on her second CD.

Nicola appears in venues all over Cornwall and her act is unforgettable.